SELF HOME REMEDIES
FROM HEAD TO TOE

PART 2 N'S TO Z

1

INTRODUCTION

My name is WANDA CHELLERS AUTHOR of WORKING INDEPENDENTLY, LETTING GO HEALS, ASSETS and LIABILITES, SELF HOME REMEDIES FROM HEAD TO TOE.
I love to write, research and type. I am retired as you can see in all my books that I have publish. I am soon to be sixty years old, one daughter by birth who is Tomika Dix forty years old, I have other daughters but not by birth because all children are ours. I have a grandson his name is Joshia who I love very much. I have to give God all the honor and praise because if it had not been for the creator of the universe I could have not made it.

Through prayer and meditation also love and blessing everything and every body, I never would have made it. In my younger years I didn't know what I have learn in my senior years. If I knew what I know now I would have already been very successful in everything I do. I have learn that anything I am fascinated whether good or evil I can draw it to myself.

Now I am ready to help the next generation to move forward in their lives. This can only happen when they are ready. How many of the senior generation know this why we are here to teach and let our light shine that men will see our good works and Glorify the Father in heaven. The word in 1 Peter 5: 2, Fellow elders, this is my plea to you: 2. Feed the flock of God; care for it willingly, not grudgingly; not for what you will get out of it, but because you are eager to serve the Lord. 5. You young men, follow the leadership of those who are older. And all of you serve each other with humble spirits, for God gives special blessings to those who are humble, but sets himself against those who are proud. I was taught to go to school and get a good education, go to college and get a good job, because this all my parents knew. I am here today to tell those who are going to college that is great, but after you get out you will have students loan and also your parents, If you didn't get a scholarship. This is my feeling today, students from Middle Schools, High Schools, Technical Schools, of Colleges should be given a trade so when they come out someone will give them an entry level job on the job training. Wow college students should have a job waiting on them in the field they are majoring in as entry level so they can get on the job training. This would be paid training so students can pay their college loans, coming out of college without a job put pressure, stress and anxiety, on students and parents. This curriculum activity should be in every school around the world and country. Teaching students along with math how to manage money so when they are out in the world, they can be a good steward over their finances. I am hoping this book will be a great help to those who want to eat, exercise and come off medication to be healthy. First we have to love ourselves, others and stop being in others and stop being in other people affairs and mind our own affairs. Pray, ask for forgiveness, forgive yourself, meditate everyday, be happy don't worry. Everything is in divine order, God word in 1 Peter 5: 7. : Let him have all your worries and cares, for he is always thinking about you and watching everything that concerns you. First Book of Self Health Home Remedies From Head To Toe A-M, the Second Book is from N-Z

PEACE AND BLESSINGS:
WANDA CHELLERS

CONTENT

CHAPTER 25 Y'S
YEAST INFECTION
TEETH YELLOW
CHAPTER 26
ZINC DEFICIENCY

CHAPTER 14 N'S

Health is like money we never have a true idea of its value until we lose it.
Josh Billings

*Nasal Crowding is blocked nose or stuffy nose, it happen when swelling of the nasal cavity is a buildup of mucus. This come when we have a cold, flu and allergic reaction.
*These are some remedies we can use: Apple Cider Vinegar a natural

decongestant to help break up congested mucous. Mix two tablespoon of raw apple cider vinegar, one tablespoon raw honey a cup of warm water, drink two to three time daily for few days.

*Cayenne Pepper is good for relieving nasal congestion also blocked sinuses. Cayenne induces a runny nose to get rid of mucus and allergens. Add half teaspoon of cayenne powder to one tablespoon of raw honey and eat it a few time daily.
*Garlic fight the respiratory infection causing congestion, boil two to three garlic clove in one cup of water. You

can mix a half teaspoon of turmeric powder, drink twice daily until the congestion clears.
*PLEASE NOTE: Always consult your doctor before taking any kind of supplement.
*Eucalyptus Oil help clear the airways of mucus, work as a natural cough suppressant, add three to five drops of eucalyptus oil to boiling water in a large pot.

Use a towel to cover the head and slowly in hale the steam through the nose for two minutes at a time. Keep your eyes closed, do this twice daily.
* More Remedies: Ginger, Turmeric

*Essential Oil For Nasal Crowding: Peppermint Oil, Tea Tree Oil,

Eucalyptus Oil, Oregano Oil, Thyme Oil, Lavender Oil, Lemon Oil, Rosemary Oil, Cinnamon Oil, Clove Oil, and Pine or Cedar Wood Oil.

*Deadness in Hand/ Feet (Numbness), deadness in the hand and feet can be due to medical conditions, such as carpal tunnel syndrome, diabetes, migraines, multiple sclerosis, and under-active thyroid.

Remedies for Deadness (Numbness) in the hand and feet, first apply a warm compress on the affected area, will increase blood supply also relax the muscles and nerves, dip a wash cloth in warm water, wring excess water out, place on affected area for five to seven minutes.

Repeat several times until the deadness or (Numbness go away).
*Exercise can improve blood circulation and oxygen to all the body.
*Eat more Vitamin B foods, foods that are high in B Vitamins, especially B 6 and B 12, good for nerve functioning and being deficiency can cause numbness in certain body parts like hands, arms, fingers and legs.

*Essential Oils: Peppermint Oil, Eucalyptus Oil, Frankincense Oil, Rosemary Oil, Lavender Oil.

*Use two drops of peppermint Oil, two drops Eucalyptus Oil, two drops of Frankincense Oil, two drops Rosemary Oil, two drops Lavender Oil, one ounce of carrier oil-

fractional coconut oil.

*Nail Growing: You can grow nails with some home remedies with simple ingredients: Olive Oil is the best when it come to caring for the nails. Olive Oil contains Vitamin E which improve circulation and grow you nails.
*Before going to bed apply warm olive oil to the nails and cuticles, massage for five minutes, wear cotton glove overnight, do once daily.

*Coconut Oil help with healthy nail growth, it strengths your cuticles, also help cure hang nails, cuticle infection and fungal on the nails. Massage your nails and hands with warm extra-virgin coconut oil daily at night before going to bed, massage in circular motions to improve blood circulation. *Stinging Nettle strengthens nails, preventing weak and brittle nail, add two to three teaspoon of dried stinging nettle leaves to a cup of hot water, cover and steep for ten minutes, strain and add honey, drink a cup of herbal tea daily.

*Essential Oils: Myrrh Oil, Lavender Oil, Lemon Oil, Frankincense Oil, Geranium Oil.

*Bleeding Nose: Nose bleeds can be brought on by nutritional deficiencies, hormonal, changes during pregnancy, upper respiratory infection, high blood pressure, blood clotting disorders and cancer.

*These are some remedies for Nose Bleeds: Pinch nose, sit with your head tiled sightly forward, use your thumb and index finger, pinch the soft part of the nose below the bony bridge, do this for five to ten minutes, as you do this breathe through your mouth. Release the pressure gently and sit quietly for five minutes, repeat as needed until bleeding stops.
*PLEASE NOTE: DON'T LAY FLAT, TILT YOUR HEAD OR PUT YOUR HEAD BETWEEN YOUR LEGS, ALSO DON'T BLOW YOUR NOSE.

*Cold Compress cause the blood vessels to constrict faster and slow down the blood flow, wrap a few ice cubes in a thin towel, sit in an up right position and tilt your head back,
apply the ice pack across the bridge of the nose for five to ten minutes, repeat as needed.
*PLEASE NOTE: DON'T APPLY ICE DIRECTLY ON YOUR NOSE.

*These are other remedies: Onion, Cayenne, Apple Cider Vinegar, Saline Water, Nettle, Coriander, Holy Basil and Petroleum Jelly.

*Essential Oils: Helichrysum Oil, Lemon Oil, Frankincense Oil, Myrrh

Oil, Geranium Oil, Rose Oil, and Lavender Oil.

CHAPTER 15 O'S

To get rich never risk your health, for it is the truth that health is the wealth of wealth.
Richard Baker

*Warning sign for Ovarian: Family history,50 or over, never given birth, menstruation early, going through menopause after 50 years old, medications certain one, smoking, ovary syndrome and obesity.
*Warning signs: Pelvic or abdominal pain, uncomfortable or painful

intercourse, abdominal bloating or swelling, frequent or urgent need to urinate, difficulty eating or getting full quickly, vaginal abnormalities, lower back pain, shortness of breath or difficulty breathing, changes in bowel habits and constant fatigue.

*Home Remedies For Oral Cancer: Leafy Vegetables, Green Tea, Raspberries, Tomatoes, Avocados, Drumsticks.
*Spices that prevent cancer: Turmeric/ Cumin, Cinnamon, Oregano, Cayenne Pepper/ Capsaicin (Chill Peppers) and Ginger.

*Essential Oils for Cancer: Citrus

Oils, Clary Sage Oil, Frankincense Oil, Lavender Oil, Lemongrass Oil, Myrrh Oil, Peppermint and Spearmint Oil, Thyme Oil and Turmeric Oil (Curcumin).

*Cysts On Ovarian can cause these symptoms: abdominal bloating, pain during bowel movements, menstrual irregularities, pelvic pain, lower back pain, pain during sex, menstrual cycle. Pain in lower back or thighs, pressure in rectum or bladder, nausea and vomiting.

*Here are some remedies for Ovarian Cysts: Heat reduce muscle cramps, pain in abdomen.
*Castor Oil Pack clear the body of excess tissues and toxins, fold a large

flannel cloth. Use two tablespoons of castor oil on the cloth, lay down with an old towel under you and put the flannel cloth on your abdomen, cover the castor oil cloth with plastic then a old towel, place the hot water bottle over the towel and cover yourself with a blanket, leave it on for at lease thirty minutes and remove, repeat three times a week for three months, wash oil with a solution of three tablespoons of baking soda one quart(four cups) water.

*Please Note: Don't USE CASTOR OIL PACK WHEN ON MENSTRUATION.

*Beetroot clear toxins out of your system, reduces the severity of many symptoms of ovarian cysts, mix one-half cup freshly beetroot juice, one tablespoon of Aloe Vera Gel and black strap molasses, drink it once daily before breakfast, do this remedy until your symptoms have reduced.

*These are more remedies: Ginger Juice, Flex-seed, Epsom Salt Bath, Chamomile Tea, Apple Cider Vinegar, Almond and Increase Fluid Intake.

*Essential Oils For Cyst On Ovarian: Geranium Oil, Lavender Oil, Sandalwood Oil, Clary Sage Oil, Cypress Oil, Cinnamon Oil, Frankincense Oil, Rose Otto Oil, German Chamomile Oil and Myrrh Oil.

*Obesity attributed to poor lifestyle, unbalanced diet, eating processed foods, high in fat, oversize food portions, over eating, excessive drinking, lack of physical activity, lack of sufficient sleep, hypothyroidism, insulin resistance, medications.

*Here are some remedies: Lemon Juice, Vitamin B and C, Calcium, Minerals, Magnesium, Iron, Zinc. Improve digestion and detoxification, Remove toxins from the body, mix three teaspoon lemon juice one teaspoon honey, one half teaspoon back pepper powder in a glass of water. If using ground black pepper just add a quarter teaspoon, drink on an empty stomach in the morning, do this daily for three months.

*Cabbage for weight loss and obesity, Protect the body from chronic diseases and decrease the risk of certain type of cancers.
*Honey and Cinnamon: Pour a cup hot water over half teaspoon of cinnamon powder can also use cinnamon sticks, let steep for one hour or a half an hour, mix one teaspoon organic honey, drink on an empty stomach in the morning a half an hour before breakfast, put the rest in the refrigerator and drink it at night before going to bed.
*These are more remedies: Apple Cider Vinegar, Green Tea, Cayenne Pepper, Curry Leaves, Tomatoes and Fennel.

*Essential Oil for Obesity: Cinnamon Oil, Ginger Oil, Lemon Oil, Peppermint Oil, Bergamot Oil, Fennel Oil, and Grapefruit Oil.

*Osteoarthritis the common form of arthritis due to the breakdown of cartilage in joint, which cause your bones to rub against each other. Symptoms are joint pain, joint stiffness, joint feel tender to the touch, loss of flexibility.
*Here are some home remedies: Exercise, Hot and Cold Compress: Hot Compress wrap a hot bottle water in a thin towel. * Cold Compress wrap a few ice cubes in a thin towel. The hot compress over the affected joint two to three

minutes, replace with the cold compress, leave on for about one minute, repeat process for fifteen to twenty minutes few time daily.
*PLEASE Note: can be use separately.

*Massage Therapy, Apple Cider Vinegar, Epsom Salt, Ginger, Turmeric, Fenugreek, Green Tea, and Cinnamon.

*Essential Oils for Osteoarthritis: Eucalyptus Oil, Frankincense Oil, Lavender Oil, Evening Primrose Oil, Ginger Oil, Turmeric Oil, and Basil Oil.
*Mix with carrier oil such as: Coconut Oil, Olive Oil, Amla Oil, Jojoba Oil, Grape-Seed Oil, Almond Oil, and Argan Oil.

CHAPTER 16P'S

Calm mind brings inner strength and self-confidence, so that's very important for good health.
Dalai Lama

Panic Attack is surge, overwhelming anxiety and intense fear, will appear without warning, symptoms come like chest pain, shortness of breath, hyperventilation, rapid heart beat, sweating, trembling, hot or cold flashes, nausea, numbness or tingling or a choking feeling in your throat.

*These are remedies to deal with it: Sit relax your muscles, breathe through your nose, breath out your mouth and stay calm in your spirit, do until you feel calm.

*Chamomile Tea help: Mix two teaspoon of chamomile in a cup of hot water, steep for ten minutes. You can add honey then drink, drink two cup of this tea daily.
*Green Tea is good for our mind and body, mix two teaspoon of green tea in a cup of hot water, steep for five minutes, you can add lemon juice and honey before you drink it, do this two to three times daily.

Essential Oil for Panic Attack: Lavender Oil, Rose Oil, Vetiver Oil, Ylang-Ylang

Oil, Bergamot Oil, Chamomile Oil, and Frankincense Oil. Aromatherapy is also good.

*Skin Peel/ Face some symptoms are Sunburn, Exposure to Harsh Climatic, no proper care for your skin, harsh skin products, allergic reaction, staying in polluted area, skin disorders and medical condition such as weak immune system, medication and dermatitis. *These are some remedies to help with the condition: Olive Oil dab olive oil on your face with your finger tips massage in your skin in circular motion, apply three time daily until you see improvement.
*Cool Compress can help if you have had a sun burn reduce

inflammation and bring relief of the pain, put ice cubes in a wash cloth and tie together, put the compress on your face for five minutes, take a break for five minutes and then repeat, use several times a day for discomfort.

PLEASE NOTE: Don't put ice directly on your sunburned skin it will worsen your condition.

*Honey reduce inflammation prevent an infection, before taking a shower use honey on your face and massage gently into your skin as you leave it on for ten minutes, wash off in your shower.
*These are more remedies: Aloe Vera,

Oatmeal, Cucumber, Banana, Water, and Milk.

*Essential Oils for Skin Peel/ Face: Helichrysum Oil, Lavender Oil, Lemongrass Oil, Lavender Tea Tree Oil, Frankincense Oil, German Chamomile Oil, Pre Diluted Rose Otto Oil.

Eye Pink: Symptoms such as pain, disturbed vision, sensitivity to light. If it will not improve, with home remedy see your doctor.

*Black Tea reduce itching and inflammation, it combat viral and bacterial infections too. Put black tea bags on your eyes for ten minutes, apply three or four times daily every

few hours. Green tea bags and
chamomile tea bags you can use.
Weak black tea bags for a solution
can be use as an eye wash.
*Eye bright: use a cup of boiling water
and let it cool then add five drops of
eye bright to it, use as an eye wash in
an eye cup.
*Breast milk: Put a few drops in your
affected eye, repeat as you need.

*These are other remedies: Honey
and milk, Aloe Vera and Boric Acid.

*Essential Oils for Pink Eye: Tea Tree
Oil, Myrrh Oil, Eucalyptus Oil, Clove
Oil, and Roman Chamomile Oil.

*Plants Positive Energy: By putting positive plants around you or your home and office it will benefit you and people around you also move negative from around you and others.
*Bamboo Plant is low in maintenance, low light, keep away from direct sunlight, keep in a glass bowl with one inch of distilled or purified water, keep bamboo stalks to odd numbers and considered to be luck.
*PLEASE NOTE: BAMBOO IS TOXIC TO DOGS AND CATS.

*Money Plant: produces positive energy, attract good luck and fortune, put this plant inside your house. It purify air polluted your house. It purify air polluted synthetic

chemicals from furniture, cleaning
solutions, filters the indoor air,
increase oxygen in flow.
*Sage Plant use to get rid of negative
emotions, such as anger and fear
from your life. Put positive energy in
your home and office.

*These are other plants that have
positive energy: Holy Basil plant,
Orchid plant, Peace Lily plant,
Rosemary plant, Jasmine plant, Aloe
Vera plant, and Chrysanthemum.

*Essential Oils for Positive Energy:
Lavender Oil, Frankincense Oil, Wild
orange, Oil, Peppermint Oil,
Bergamot Oil, Ylang-Ylang Oil,
Vetiver Oil, Sandalwood Oil,
Rosemary Oil, and Roman
Chamomile Oil.

CHAPTER 17 Q' S

It is health that is real wealth and not pieces of gold and silver.
Mahatma Gandhi

*Smoking (Quit) can cause many health problems such as respiratory problems, high blood pressure, increase in heart rate, weaken your immune system, low sperm count in men, reduce fertility in women, irregular menstrual cycle, early menopause, lung and other type of cancer.

*These are remedies to quit smoking: Licorice help with balance cortisol levels, reduce fatigue and restore your energy. Drink this at lease two or three times a day.

*** PLEASE NOTE: IF YOU HAVE DIABETES, HIGH BLOOD PRESSURE, ADRENAL DISEASE OR REDUCED KIDNEY OR LIVER FUNCTIONING DON'T TAKE, CONSULT YOUR DOCTOR.**

*Cayenne Pepper: You can use fresh pepper, ground pepper powder, capsules or tea to quit smoking. Take a pinch of cayenne pepper to a glass of water, drink daily whenever you have a strong desire to smoke.
*Acupuncture can help you quit smoking, instills a sense of calm if you are going through withdrawal, help with the detoxification process.

You may want to go get frequent acupuncture sessions for your first two weeks.

*These are other remedies to stop smoking: Ear massage, Valerian, Passion flower, and Lobelia.

*Essential Oils to Quit Smoking: Black Pepper Oil, Angelica Oil, Lavender Oil, Chamomile Oil, Bergamot Oil, Citrus Oils, and Ylang-Ylang Oil.

CHAPTER 18 R'S

**Under Breast Rash: The cause of rash under the breast is excessive sweating, heat, lack of air circulation and a tight fitting bra that come against your breasts.
*These are home remedies you might want to use: Cotton Ball place a piece between the lower part of the breasts to absorb moisture. Wear light weight clothing made of cotton.
*Cornstarch keep the skin dry. If you have a rash use talc because fungi feed on cornstarch. Clean area with soap and water then pat with towel, then light dust with cornstarch, do twice a day until the problem is gone.**

***PLEASE NOTE: DON'T PUT CORNSTARCH ON MOIST OR WET SKIN**

***Coconut Oil will help provide relief from rashes, it reduce friction that cause rashes under your breasts avoid infection, apply extra-virgin coconut oil on your affected area, let it absorb completely in to your skin, use it two to three times a day until your rash is gone.**
***Other remedies are : Calamine Lotion, Tea Tree Oil, Aloe Vera, Garlic, Lemon.**
***Essential Oils for Rash Under Breast: Tea Tree Oil, Lavender Oil, Geranium Oil, Rosemary Oil, Rose Oil, Peppermint Oil, Sandalwood Oil,**

Cedar Wood Oil, and Myrrh Oil.

*Nose Runny is a common cold, sinus infection, allergic reaction and a change in the weather outside.

*These are some remedies to use: Steam, hold your face over a bowl of hot water with a towel over your face, breathe for at lease ten minutes, try this three or four times daily. Eucalyptus oil or menthol is good to put in the hot water. *Eucalyptus Oil can give you relief from your running nose, put a large bowl of hot water, add seven drops of eucalyptus oil and four drops of lavender oil, peppermint oil to the water, cover your head with a towel

and inhale the steam, use this two
to three times a day.
*Honey help reduce the symptoms
of a runny nose, put a table spoon
of honey in a cup, a pinch of
cinnamon powder and one half
tablespoon of lemon juice, mix
twice a day, mix two teaspoon of
honey in a glass of warm water and
drink twice daily.

*Basil has a strong healing
properties that warm the body
inside also treat runny nose, chew
three or four basil leaves before
breakfast also before going to bed,
use eight to ten basil leaves, five
cloves to a cup of water, let it boil for
ten minutes, add sugar, let it cool
and drink, use it twice a day.

*Other remedies are: Cayenne Pepper, Garlic, Ginger, Turmeric, Mustard Oil, Steam, and Salt Water.

*Essential Oils for Nose Running: Lavender Oil, Sandalwood, Frankincense and Ravensara Oils, Eucalyptus Oil, Tea Tree Oil, Peppermint Oil and Lemon Oil.

*Ringworm is cause by fungi on the top layer of the skin feed on keratin in the skin, thrive in warm moist areas, it cause round, scaly patches, darker border shape of a ring and accompanied by redness, itching and inflammation on skin.
*These are some remedies to use: Neem help treat ringworm, scabies, various infections of your

skin, apply Neem Oil on the area once or twice a day, try applying one half teaspoon of Neem Oil and one cup of Aloe Vera Gel. You can also use equal part of crushed Neem leaves, turmeric powder and sesame oil, apply this paste on the area of the ringworm.

*I dine: use two percent iodine solution, don't use for more than three days.

*Wash the area with antibacterial soap and dry with a clean towel, soak a cotton ball or swab in iodine tincture, dab on the affected area, use this twice or three times a day for three or four weeks.

*Papaya help kill fungi that cause ringworm, rub a slice of raw papaya on area, leave on for at lease fifteen minutes, and rinse with warm water use two times a day a few days.

*Essential Oils for Ringworm: Tea Tree Oil, Coconut Oil, Turmeric Oil, Aloe Vera Oil, Oregano Oil, and Lemon Oil.

*Arthritis (Rheumatoid) symptoms for rheumatoid arthritis is muscle and joint pain swelling morning stiffness, and fatigue.

*These are some remedies to help: Fish Oil, include Cold Water Fish, like Salmon, Tuna in your diet.

*PLEASE NOTE: Check with your doctor before taking fish oil supplements, because it may interfere with some medications your are taking.

*Garlic is good for rheumatoid arthritis, use raw and fresh garlic, eat one to two raw garlic cloves daily. You can also use capsules for correct dosage consult your doctor.

*Evening Primrose can reduce pain and morning stiffness. Ask your doctor to get the correct dosage because it may interfere with other medications.
*Massage will stimulate blood circulation which will alleviate discomfort and inflammation in joints.

You can add some drops of lavender oil to warm olive oil and massage the area very gentle strokes. Massage the area two to three times daily a few minutes.

*PLEASE NOTE: AVOID MASSAGE IF YOUR JOINT AND MUSCLES ARE TOO TENDER

*Essential Oils for Rheumatoid Arthritis: Frankincense Oil, Lavender Oil, Evening Primrose Oil, Ginger Oil, Turmeric Oil, and Basil Oil

CHAPTER 19 S'S

*Shingles is a skin rash with pain and burning sensation. Anyone who had chicken-pox can get shingles. If you are elderly who have had chicken-pox can get shingles. If you are elderly who have had chicken-pox before one year old are at higher risk, weak immune systems, cancer, lymphoma, immunodeficiency virus and leukemia will be at high risk of shingles. Symptom of shingles are headache, fever, body pain, fatigue also sensitive to light. *Here are some home remedies for Shingles: Cold water can help with pain

blisters, put towel in cold water,
take out excess water, place on
blisters, let it stay for twenty
minutes and take off, you can
repeat until pain decrease.

*PLEASE NOTE: DON'T USE ICE
PACKS OR WATER TOO COLD.

*Licorice help in the treatment of
shingles, one teaspoon of licorice
powder to make paste, apply on
affected area, let dry and rinse with
warn water, do this two to three times
per day for one to two weeks

*Lemon Balm: will help to get rid of
pain, discomfort from blisters and
rashes, drink this tea steeping two to
four teaspoons of the herb in one cup

boiling water for ten minutes, let cool, soak cotton ball in tea, apply on the affected area, leave on to dry, continue to repeat four times a day until you get relief.

Essential Oils for Shingles: Tea Tree Oil, Lavender Oil, Geranium Oil, Clove Oil, Oregano Oil, Peppermint Oil, Lemon Balm Oil, Ravensara Oil, Bergamot Oil, Chamomile Oil.

*Sinus Infection often come by a cold that will cause swelling, inflammation and will lead to mucus buildup that block the sinuses. Symptoms for sinus are, facial tenderness, pain, pressure, nasal stuffiness, nasal discharge, sore throat, cough and a fever.

*These are some home remedies for Sinus Infection: Cayenne Pepper open up, drain your sinuses. Boosts immunity, reduces swelling, inflammation, improves circulation, mix one teaspoon cayenne pepper a cup of hot water, drink two or three times daily.

*Onion open up sinuses and will fight bacteria and fungi. Chop onion put pieces in a pot of water, let boil five minutes and inhale for a few minutes, strain the liquid and drink it, repeat a few time daily for a week or until your congestion clears.

*Horseradish help remove mucus from the nasal passages, us a pinch of freshly grated horseradish in your mouth, hold in mouth until its flavor dissipates, then swallow, repeat a few time daily about one week or until your infection clears up.

*Essential Oil for Sinus Infection: Lemon Oil, Eucalyptus Oil, Peppermint Oil, Lavender Oil, Oregano Oil, Rosemary Oil, Chamomile Oil and Tea Tree Oil

*Armpit Skin Tags form and appear on your skin creases, friction that occur, painless will get irritated by your clothing, jewelry which can increase the risk of infection. These are the risk factors such as being female, increasing age, obesity,

genetics, certain endocrine syndromes, metabolic syndrome and hormonal imbalances.
*These are remedies for skin Tag Armpits: Dental floss can remove any skin tags on neck you can use for armpits.

*Wash underarm mild soap, pat dry, use rubbing alcohol on your skin, tie dental floss as tightly around the bottom of your skin tag, cover tag with a bandage, everyday sterilize with alcohol, and change bandage, with one to two weeks, tag will wither and fall off on your skin.

*Tea Tree Oil help treat your skin disorders and skin tags will dry out your skin tags cause it to fall off, use three drops on cotton ball,putcotton

ball on your skin and after secure
with a bandage, leave on for one
hour remove and rinse the area
with warm water, repeat once or
twice daily for a week until it
vanishes from the skin.

*Please Note: If you are sensitive to
tea tree oil dilute the oil with equal
water and oil before using it.

*Iodine help break down the built-up
skin cells will cause it to fall off, clean
your under arms mild soap, take a
cotton swab and dip in to the iodine,
apply to skin tag, cover with a
bandage, do this daily until the tag
come off.

*Essential Oil for Skin Tags: Australian Tea Tree Oil, Oregano Oil, Frankincense Oil, Castor Oil, Lavender Oil, Rose Hip Seed Oil, Lemon Oil, Sweet Basil Oil.

*Stoke(Signs) These are some signs of a stroke, numbness in arm, leg, face or one side of the body. Trouble walking, balance and coordination, trouble speaking, understanding people speaking. * These herbal supplements may improve blood circulation: Indian Ginseng, Ashwagandha has antioxidant properties that prevent and treat stroke, these are more herbs such as Bilberry, Garlic, Asian Ginseng, Gotu- Kola and Turmeric.

***Essential Oil for Stroke: Frankincense Oil, Geranium Oil, Helichrysum Oil, Lavender Oil, Lemon Oil, Peppermint Oil, Lemon, Peppermint Oil, Rosemary Oil, and Sandalwood Oil.**

CHAPTER 20 T'S

Take care of your body. It's the only place you have to live.
Jim Rohn

*Teeth/ Gums to keep you teeth and gums healthy we must keep a healthy oral hygiene such as brushing your teeth at least twice a day, flossing once or twice a day, flossing once or twice a day, rinse your mouth after each meal and use mouth wash once a day.
*Here are some remedies to help keep your teeth and gums healthy. Oil pulling detoxifies and cleanses the body it is good for oral and over all health, use one teaspoon sesame oil in mouth, do this for twenty minutes, spit it out after swish it

around in your mouth, rinse with warm water using salt water, brush your teeth, do it in the morning on an empty stomach.
*Another oil to use is coconut oil.
*Guava Leaves are effective in treating periodontal disease, help maintain strong teeth as well as gums. You can chew after washing leaves good, then spit out, grind the leave use as toothpaste to bush your teeth.

*Green tea destroy bacteria that cause you to have tooth decay, cavities and gum disease.

*Essential Oils for Teeth/ Gums: Cinnamon Oil, Clove Oil, Eucalyptus Oil, Myrrh Oil Lavender Oil, Lemon Oil, Peppermint Oil, and Spearmint Oil

*Grinding Teeth are cause by stress, suppressed anger, frustration, misaligned teeth. The growth of your teeth and jaws also much more.

*These are some remedies you can use: Valerian help muscle to relax and you can enjoy sleep, mix few drops of Valerian Oil with one teaspoon of olive oil then massage on jaw also neck area, you can also drink Valerian Tea if you would like.

*Lavender calm and soothing the nervous, also reduce relaxation and help you to sleep better at night, mthree to four drops lavender oil ,one teaspoon of almond oil or olive oil. You can use this oil to massage jaw and neck, do this during the day and at bedtime.

*Essential Oils for Teeth Grinding: Peppermint Oil, Frankincense Oil, Lavender Oil, Chamomile Oil, Valerian Oil, Rosemary Oil, Turmeric Oil, Ylang-Ylang Oil, Clary Sage Oil, Rose Oil, Bergamot Oil, Geranium Oil *Thyroid Problem these are most common thyroid problems, Hypothyroidism (under-active thyroid), hyperthyroidism (over-active thyroid), these are most common can cause hormonal, emotional and physical changes in your body.

*These are some of the problem that will appear: Felling fatigued, sudden change with your body weight, depression, anxiety, menstrual problems, sudden hair loss and feeling cold or hot, hoarse voice, discomfort in your neck, bowel problems, skin dryness and muscle and joint pain.
*Essential Oils for Thyroid Problems: Over-active Thyroid Oils: Lavender Oil, Wintergreen Oil, Sandalwood Oil, Pine Oil.
*Under-active Thyroid: Spearmint Oil, Peppermint Oil, Myrrh Oil, Rose Geranium Oil, and Cedar Wood Oil.

*Tuberculosis: TB is highly contagious, respiratory infection that is cause by bacteria. Symptoms are: Fatigue,persistent coughing, shortness of breath, weight loss, night sweats, fever also sensation of pain in your chest, kidneys also back.

*These are some remedies to use: Garlic destroys the germs causing TB which you can eat it raw or cooked, mix one half teaspoon chop garlic and a cup of milk with four cups of water, boil until it is reduce to one fourth in size, then drink it three time a day.

*Indian Gooseberry give you energy and body capacity to function. DE-Seed three or four gooseberries, extract the juice using a juicer, add one tablespoon honey, drink every morning on empty stomach. *Oranges can boot your immune system, protect the body from secondary infections, add a pinch of salt, one teaspoon honey to a glass fresh squeeze orange juice, drink twice daily, a glass in the morning, a glass in the evening.

*Essential Oils for Tuberculosis: Eucalyptus Oil, Frankincense Oil, Peppermint, and Thieves Oil.

CHAPTER 21 U'S

Health is the crown on the well person's head that only the ill person can see.
Robin Sharma

*Urinary Tract Infection: Occurs when your bladder and exit tuber are infected with bacteria also the causes are sexual intercourse, wait to long to urinate, pregnancy, menopause, and diabetes. Symptoms can be such as urinated frequent, pass a small amount of urine, burning sensation when your urinating, change in your urine color and abdominal pain, also fever, nausea also vomiting.

*Remedies you can use to treat Urinary Tract Infection: Cranberry Juice prevent bacteria from reaching the walls in the urethra that causes urinary tract infection, drink half glass cranberry juice daily to prevent urinary tract infection, if you are suffering with urinary tract infection you can drink three to four glasses of cranberry juice to prevent infection from causing damage to your kidney's

*PLEASE NOTE: DRINK UNSWEETENED CRANBERRY JUICE.*PLEASE NOTE: DON'TDRINKCRANBERRY JUICE IF YOUHAVE OR SUFFER WITH KIDNEYSTONES.

*Baking Soda will give you relief from the pain and will speed up the recovery, add one teaspoon of baking soda to a glass of water and drink once or twice daily.

*Ova Ursi help fight infection, you can get this herb in supplement form. When you take Uva Ursi it kill the bacteria and stimulates urination.
*Stomach upset can be cause by poisoning, infection, allergic reaction, over eating, stress, drinking to much, motions sickness, medication side effect, pregnancy and gastrointestinal disease. Systems can be abdominal bloating, loose stools, cramps, heart burn, chills, vomiting and nausea.

66

*These are some home remedies to try: Bananas will treat loose stools, indigestion and gastrointestinal problems. Bananas help absorb excess acid in your stomach, mash ripe banana, mix in a glass of buttermilk, drink two to three time daily.

*Fenugreek Seeds help bulk up the stool and give you instant relief in your stomach, put in your mouth one teaspoon of fenugreek seeds powder with one tablespoon o yogurt two to three times daily for relief.
*Chamomile relaxes the smooth muscle lining in the digestive tract, can help improve your upset digestive system quickly, mix one teaspoon each of

chamomile flowers with peppermint leaves with one cup of water., after straining add a teaspoon of honey, drink it three times daily, you can also use per-packaged tea bags.

Essential Oils for stomach upset: Peppermint Oil, Clay Oil, Lemon Balm Oil, Chamomile Oil, Eucalyptus Oil, Ginger Oil, Fennel Oil, Cinnamon Oil, and Lemon Oil.

Vaginal Cysts form when you gland or duct start clogged causing liquid. These are the four different vaginal cysts. 1) Inclusion Cysts is small and are in the back of your virginal wall. 2) Bartholin's Cysts is a fluid-filled cysts. 3) Gartner's duct cysts which don't disappear as they are to, after you have a baby. 4) Mullerian Cysts is form when a baby develops. A vaginal cyst is rarely cancerous, and will not cause you discomfort, cyst are discovered when you have a routine pelvic exam.

*These are some home remedies to treat vaginal cysts: Sitz Bath reduce the discomfort of vaginal cysts and

will help reduce infection, alleviate irritation help heal, fill the tub with warm water, use one to two tablespoon of epsom salt in the water, soak just the genital area fifteen minutes or until the water loses heat, pat dry do this two to three times daily for one week.
*Please Note: you may want to buy a sitz bath kit to put over your toilet set to use.

*Apple Cider Vinegar help reduce the size and swelling of the vaginal cysts, pour a cup of raw unfiltered apple cider vinegar with a glass of warm water, soak the lower bottom for fifteen minutes, do two to three times daily. You can also add one teaspoon of this apple cider vinegar with a glass of water drink it twice a day to help with healing within your body.

*Tea Tree Oil help pain and inflammation that come with vaginal cysts, good for treating bartholin cysts, help with harmful bacteria in your vaginal, help drain the cyst with in one or two days, use two to three drops one hundred percent tea tree oil and two teaspoon of coconut oil, using a cotton ball apply on the cyst. Leave for twenty minutes and rinse with warm water. Use this remedy once to twice daily or as you need it. You can also add three to five drops tea tree oil a cup of water to rinse the area a few times a day.

Essential Oils for Vaginal Cysts: Bergamot Oil, German Chamomil Oil, Lavender Oil, and Tea Tree Oil.

*Order In Vaginal can be cause by bacterial growth yeast infections, poor hygiene, hormonal changes also sexually transmitted diseases. You may have redness, itching, burning also irritation in your vaginal area, a fishy odor down in your vaginal area.

*These are some remedies to get rid of the odor: Baking soda will help balance your pH level, use one half cup of baking soda to bath water, soak for twenty minutes, will fight a yeast infection, help get rid of odor quickly.

*Yogurt restore the normal vaginal pH level, when the pH level is balance the   vaginal odor is gone, eat two cups unsweetened plain yogurt a day, you can also use probiotic supplements.

*White Vinegar will neutralize the odor breaking down odor proteins. Do a white vinegar rinse will eliminate vaginal odor, help restore pH balance level, use one half cup white vinegar and salt equal in Luke warm water in bath, soak for a few minutes, do this several times weekly.

*Essential Oils for Vaginal Odor: Tea Tree Oil.

*Vitamin B12 Deficiency can occur due to diet that don't have enough of B12. This vitamin is found in animal products, one more cause is pernicious anemia. We are at a high risk at age fifty or older, if you are a vegetarian or vegan diet, infants born to vegan mothers and exclusively breastfed, if you are suffering for a disease that affect digestion, such as celiac and Crohn's disease, if you have had gastrointestinal surgery, malnutrition , and chronic alcoholics.

*These are sign Of B12 Deficiency: Fatigue, low energy, numbness and tingling sensation, low blood pressure, skin lesions, depression, cognitive decline, hypothyroidism, and infertility.

*Vitamin Deficiency when you do not get enough sunlight also don't eat enough foods rich in vitamin D, we are at higher risk in suffering with vitamin D deficiency, if we have dark skin are over fifty years old and if we live in a place where there are long period of darkness then we can have vitamin D deficiency. To increase our level of vitamin D we have to expose ourselves to sun and eat a diet high in vitamin D. One way is to exposure to early morning sunlight for ten to fifteen minutes, we can get this from food such as fish, cod liver oil, egg yolks also fortified dairy and grain products, take a vitamin supplement, after consulting your doctor.

***These are signs that you have Vitamin D Deficiency: Impaired immunity, bone pain, tiredness and fatigue, mood swings, psoriasis, digestive problem, excessive sweating, high blood pressure , and overweight.**

CHAPTER 23 W'S

**The first wealth is health.
Ralph Waldo Emerson**

*Warts is a virus picked up from someone else, the common warts are flat warts, and plantar warts. They will disappear within the period of six to two years.
*These are some home remedies you can use for warts: Basil crush fresh basil leaves, rub the leaves on your warts and cover with a bandage, repeat twice a day.
*Please Note: If these remedies don't help seek a doctor for some advice.

*Banana Peel dissolve your warts and help your immune system fight

your virus, use a piece of banana peel and tape over the wart.
Do this regularly at bedtime, leave it on overnight while you sleep, use green banana peels than yellow ripe ones.

*Tea Tree Oil has great ingredient to treat and help your warts, dilute this oil because it's very strong ,dilute with water or Aloe Vera Gel so you can use it on your skin, do this several times daily and at night at bedtime, it will absorb and fight your virus.

*Essential Oils For Warts: Neem Oil, Tea Tree Oil, Cinnamon Bark Oil, Oregano Oil, Frankincense Oil, Clove Oil, and Cypress Oil.

*Wheezing can cause tightness in the chest, lack of energy, reduced oxygen in
your body. It will occur with health issues like acute bronchitis, asthma, C O P D, fluid buildup in your air sacs of your lungs. First you need to find out the underlying cause to treat the problem.

*These are home remedies to treat Wheezing: Hot shower and steam therapy will make you more comfortable, help stop your wheezing, hot shower will relax tense in your air way, the moisture help thin mucus that are clogging them. Run your hot shower with the door close this will seem like a sauna, stand in your shower for ten minutes, keeping your door close, do two to three times daily.

*Apple cider vinegar help flush out toxins and support the respiratory system, use two tablespoons of raw unfiltered vinegar with a cup of water warm, one teaspoon raw honey, drink twice a day.

*Garlic help stop wheezing also treat asthma and coughing, use three to four clove garlic boil in one cup of water or milk, let cool before you drink it for two to three times daily.

Essential Oils for Wheezing: Eucalyptus Oil, Lavender Oil, Roman Chamomile Oil, Bergamot Oil, Frankincense Oil, Oregano Oil,

Clove Oil, Tea Tree Oil, Basil Oil, and Ginger Oil.

***Whooping Cough has the same symptoms as a common cold, such as a mild cough, sneezing, runny nose and low fever.**
***PLEASE NOTE: IF YOUR INFANT IS SUFFERING IN BREATHING AND VOMITING SEEK A DOCTOR!!!!!!!!**

***These are some home remedies for Whooping Cough: Turmeric is an immune boosting that help our body fight the infection. You can mix one tablespoon raw honey and one fourth to a half of turmeric powder, take twice a day until you feel better.**

*Oregano will help clear mucus from the lungs also ease dry cough, use a pan of boiling water and add five to six drops of pure oregano oil to the water cover head with your towel, inhale two to three times daily a few days so to ease coughing.

*Lemon reduce thickness of mucus and fight infection also boosts the immune system, use one tablespoon of lemon juice, make sure it's fresh, in a glass of water warm, honey raw, drink it for several times a day, a few days.

*Essential Oil For Whooping Cough: Tea Tree Oil, Camphor Oil, Eucalyptus Oil,

Lavender Oil, Chamomile Oil, and Peppermint Oil.

*PLEASE NOTE: CAMPHOR OIL, EUCALYPTUS OIL AND PEPPERMINT SHOULD NOT BE USED WITH CHILDREN YOUNGER THAN 10 YEARS OLD.

*Wrinkles can be cause by exposure to sunlight or harsh environments, smoking, certain drugs, excessive stress, weight loss, loss of vitamin E.

*These are home remedies for Wrinkles Olive Oil fight skin damaging free radicals, Olive Oil will regenerate skin cells and keep skin

moisturized, mix a few drops of
honey, few drops olive oil

and glycerin, massage, mix put on
your skin twice a day will get rid of
dead cells
help tighten sagged skin.

*Almonds has fiber, vitamin E, iron,
zinc, calcium, folic acid and more,
which will delay your aging process
also treat your wrinkles. You can
soak almonds in raw milk over
night, remove the next morning and
grind it in a thick past. Apply on
your skin, and under eye, let stay for
twenty or thirty minutes then wash
off with warm water, you can do this
once a day.

Carrots help keep your skin smooth a good source of vitamin A, boil two to three carrots until it become soft, blend with honey to make a paste, apply to face and leave on skin a half an hour, rinse off with warm water.

*Essential Oils For Wrinkles: Helichrysum Oil, Frankincense Oil, Lavender Oil, Patchouli Oil, Rose Oil, Sandalwood Oil, Myrrh Oil, Geranium Oil, Rosemary Oil, Lemon Oil, Neroli Oil, and Carrot Seed Oil.

CHAPTER 24 X

A healthy mind does not speak ill of others.
Anonymous

X- Ray are linked to an increased risk of cancer, low risk of short-term side effects. Exposure to high radiation levels can have a range of effects, such as vomiting, bleeding, fainting, hair loss, of skin and hair. X-rays can cause mutations in our D N A and, therefore, might lead to cancer later in life. For this reason, X-rays are classified as a carcinogen by both the world health organization and the United State Government. The benefits of X-ray technology far out weight the potential negative consequence of using them.

*Benefits, the fact that X- rays have been used in medicine for such a length of time shows how beneficial they are considered to be. An X-ray alone is not always sufficient to diagnose a disease or condition, they are an essential part of the diagnostic process.
*The main benefits: Non-invasive: An x-ray can help diagnose a medical issue or monitor treatment procession without the need to physically enter and examine a patient.
*Guiding: X-ray can help guide medical professionals as they insert

catheters, stents, or other devices inside the patient. They can also help in the treatment of tumors and remove blood clots or other similar blockages. *Unexpected Finds: An X-ray can sometimes show up a feature or pathology that is different from the initial reason for the imaging. For instance, infections in the bone, gas or fluid in areas where there should be none, or some type of tumor. X-ray is here to stay.

CHAPTER 25 Y'S

**When diet is wrong, medicine is of no use. When diet is correct, medicine is of no need.
Ayurvedic Peoverb**

*Yeast Infection come when you have stress, pregnancy, health condition diabetes, taking oral contraceptive, steroids also antibiotics will cause you to have a yeast infection. Yeast can come after menopause because of your estrogen level decline. Here are some signs you could have a yeast infection itching, burning or swelling in around affected area.

*Here are some remedies that could help your yeast infection:

*Yogurt use plain yogurt, unsweetened kind, use plain yogurt on your affected area on your skin, let it stay for twenty or thirty minutes or overnight, help relieve the itching.
*Boric Acid: Please Note: Boric Acid is not to be use by pregnant women. Dilute the Boric Acid with water, apply over your affected skin, leave it on for a few minutes, rinse this area good with water, use this day by day for about two weeks.

*Oregano Oil is very good oil to boost the immune system, use oil on the

affected area of the skin. You should dilute this oil with olive oil before putting it on the skin area, you can alternate and take one or two capsules of oregano oil two times a day. You can do one of these home remedy for a few weeks to get rid of the yeast infection.
Essential Oils For Yeast Infection: Tea Tree Oil, Thyme Oil, Peppermint Oil, Clove Oil, Oregano Oil, Cinnamon Oil, Lavender Oil, and Lemongrass Oil.

*Teeth Yellow come when we are aging, poor dental hygiene, coffee, tobacco or cigarettes, high doses antibiotics, and infection.
*These are home remedies to try to help with teeth yellowing:

*Baking Soda will help remove plague from your teeth, mix teaspoon baking soda with your tooth pate, brush teeth and rinse with warm water, you can do this once or twice a week.

*Strawberries has vitamin C that will help get your teeth white, grind strawberries in a paste, rub on your

teeth, you can do twice a day or a few weeks the yellow will go away.
*Charcoal has a powerful crystal based chemical for whitens teeth, mix charcoal powder and regular tooth paste and brush your teeth, do this remedy twice a day to whiten your teeth.

***PLEASE NOTE: IF YOU DON'T HAVE ANY CHARCOAL, USE THE ASHES OF BURNT BREAD, BURNT ROSEMARY TO WHITEN YOUR TEETH !!!!!!!!**

***Essential Oils For Yellow Teeth: Lemon Oil, Sweet Orange Oil, Peppermint Oil, and Wintergreen Oil**

CHAPTER 26 Z

If you have health, you have health and happiness, you have all the wealth you need, even if it is not all you want.
Elbert Hubbard

*Zinc Deficiency is because we have insufficient nutrition, and can be due to alcoholism, bariatric surgery, diabetes. Zinc deficiency come about in young children, pregnant women, breast feeding, and elderly person.
*These are some signs of poor zinc deficiency: Persistent diarrhea, loss appetite, poor growth in our children, thinning hair, skin

problems, behavioral
disturbances, vision problems,
low cognitive function, and
week bone and joints.

*Zinc plays a key role in learning
and memory.
*Please Note: Don't over take a
large amount of zinc because it
could cause you to have nausea,
vomiting, loss of appetite,
abdominal cramps, diarrhea also
headaches. Zinc in your body can
reduce depression and anxiety,
when we don't have enough zinc in
our body we will suffer from
infection, common cold also the
flu, we can also suffer from weight
loss, loss of appetite which I have
said before. It can prevent our
children from healthy height and

weight; will cause delay sexual maturation. Zinc deficiency weaken our scalp cells, lead to alopecia, loss of pigment, dryness, brittleness. Our eye brows as well as our eyelashes can be affected, by eating zinc foods or taking zinc supplements can help with hair problem.

*Please Note: Consult your doctor before taking supplements.
*To treat skin problems use zinc-based creams, lotions on your skin for acne aging skin, herpes simplex infections, as promoting wound healing. Zinc Deficiency can result in poor night vision, cloudy cataracts. Please Note:

Consult your doctor to take supplements.

***These are some good Foods Sources: Red meat, poultry and eggs, oysters, crab, lobster, shell-fish, baked beans, chick peas, legumes, nuts, seed like cashews, almonds, sesame seeds, pumpkin seeds, whole-grain cereals, cheese and low-fat milk.**

*BONUS ONE

SAFE ESSENTIAL OILS FOR CHILDREN:

*Colds: Dilute 1-2 drops of Rosemary or Lemon in 2 TBSP of carrier oil and massage a little on neck and chest.

*CONSTIPATION: Dilute 1-2 drops of Rosemary, Ginger or Sweet Orange in a TBSP of carrier oil and massage on stomach and feet.

*CUTS & Scrapes: Add 5 drops of lavender and 5 drops of Tea Tree (melaleuca) to warm water, use to clean the wound. Apply 1 drop of Lavender to a band-aid and cover the wound. The Lavender may sting if applied directly.

*EARACHE: Apply Tea Tree (melalueca) and Lavender to the outside of ear or apply a drop of each to a cotton ball and set in the ear. Do not apply oils directly into the ear canal.

*FEVER: Dilute a drop of Lavender and a drop of Peppermint in 2 TBSP of carrier oil and massage a small amount on back of neck, behind the ears and on the back.

*FLU: Dilute 1 drop of cypress or Lemon in an unscented bath gel and use in a warm bath.

*MINOR BURNS: COOL burn first with cold water. If the skin is not broken apply 2 drops of Lavender directly to the burn. If the skin is broken apply the lavender on the perimeter of the burned area.

Apply 5 drops of Lavender to a cold, DRY cloth and gently hold over burned area.

*SUNBURN: Add 5 drops of Lavender to 1 tsp. Of Aloe Vera and apply to sunburned area. Other safe essential oils commonly used for children: Frankincense, Geranium, Sandalwood, Mandarin, Grapefruit, and Ylang-Ylang.
*Nutrient-rich virgin Coconut Oil is excellent as a carrier oil.

BONUS TWO

SAFE ESSENTIAL OILS FOR BABIES:

*COLDS: Tea Tree (melaleuca), Lemon, or Lavender. Diffuse 2 drops of either at bedtime or during the day. Mix 1 drop of either with 1 TBSP of carrier oil and massage the upper chest and back at each diaper change.

*COLIC: Mix 1 drop of Lavender with 1 TBSP of carrier oil. Gently massage a few drops into the abdomen in a clockwise direction following the natural movement of the colon.

CONSTIPATION: Lavender or Roman Chamomile. Add a drop of either to 1

TBSP of carrier oil and massage in a clockwise motion on the tummy.

COUGHS: Mix 1 drop of Lavender with 1 TBSP of carrier oil and rub a small amount on the chest and back.

CRYING: Place a small drop Lavender or Roman Chamomile on Your hand or a tissue and just let the baby smell the oil.

DIARRHEA: Mix 1 drop of Roman Chamomile with 1 TBSP of carrier oil, gently massage 2-3 drops on the tummy in a clockwise motion following the natural movement of the colon.

*DIAPER RASH: Combine 1 drop of Roman Chamomile and 1 drop of Lavender with 1 drop of whole milk. Add to baby's bath water and swish around before bathing baby. Keep the oils away from baby's eyes.

*FEVER: mix 1 drop of Lavender with 1 TBSP of carrier oil. Massage a small amount onto the bottoms of the feet and apply to the back of the neck and behind the ears, cover the feet with socks.

*JAUNDICE: Mix 1 drop of Geranium with 1 TBSP of carrier oil. Apply to the bottoms of feet and over the liver area. Do not apply oils within ½ hr before or after UVA bili-light treatment.

*TEETHING: Mix 1 drop of Roman Chamomile or Lavender with a TBSP of carrier oil. Use a small amount gently massage outside of the face along the jaw line.

*TUMMY ACHE: Mix 1 drop of Roman Chamomile and 1 drop of Sweet Orange with 2 TBSP of carrier oil.

Add 1 tsp. Of mixture to warm bath water, swishing around before bathing baby. Avoid getting oils in baby's eyes.

*Nutrient-rich virgin Coconut Oil is excellent as a carrier oil for all the safe essential oils listed here.

BONUS THREE

FIVE FINGER PRAYER

1. Your thumb is nearest to you. So begin your prayers by praying for those closest to you. These are the easiest to remember to pray for our love ones as a sweet duty.
2. The next finger is the pointing finger, pray for those who teach, instruct and heal. The includes teachers, doctors, and ministers. They need support and wisdom in pointing others in the right direction. Keep them in your prayers.
3. The next finger is the tallest finger, which reminds our leaders. Pray for the national leaders,

Leaders in business and industry, and administrators. These people shape our nation and guide public opinion. They need God's Guidance.

4. The fourth finger is our ring finger. Surprising to many is fact that this is our weakest finger, as any piano teacher will testify. It should remind us to pray for those who are weak, in trouble or in pain. They need your prayers day and night.

5. And lastly come our little finger, the smallest finger of all. Which is where we should place ourselves in relation to God and other? As the Bible says, the least shall be the greatest among you. You

pinkie should remind you to pray for yourself. B the time you have prayed for the other four groups, you own needs will be put into proper perspective. You'll be able to pray for yourself more effectively.

Some one accurately said that maturity in prayer occurs when we are able to move from the plea, Give me to the deeper prayer, and use me.

***PRAYER OF FAVORS!!!!!!!!**

Dear heart of Jesus: In the past, I have asked for many favors. This time, I ask you this very special one(   ) take it dear Jesus and place it with in your own broken heart, where your father sees it. Then in your merciful eyes, it will become your favor, not mine. Amen
(Say this three days)

AUTHOR : WANDA CHELLERS, BE

BLESS

$$$$$$$$

109

NOTES:

NOTES:

NOTES:

NOTES:

NOTES:

NOTES: